HIGHLY FLAMMABLE

A 40-Day Devotional To Help

Re-Ignite Your Passion

STEVE UPPAL

RIVER
PUBLISHING

River Publishing & Media Ltd
Bradbourne Stables
East Malling
Kent
ME19 6DZ
United Kingdom

info@river-publishing.co.uk

MIX
Paper from
responsible sources
FSC
www.fsc.org
FSC® C117931

978-1-908393-76-0
Cover design by www.spiffingcovers.com
Printed in the United Kingdom

DEDICATION

I have been greatly inspired and provoked by the lives of faithful servants of God in history. I appreciate their singleness of focus, commitment and dedication to Jesus Christ in the face of much opposition. I dedicate this book to all those who have paid the price to live a no-compromise life, and have fuelled their fire for the Lord each and every day.

INTRODUCTION

A Life of Fire

The family were still sleeping, and I was quietly leaving the holiday apartment where we were staying, when the Holy Spirit whispered a question into my heart:

"Is it possible to live in a fiery way at all times – and for this Fire to be steadily growing in intensity, heat, light, and roaring?"

The question caught me off guard. As I drove to the coffee shop, it replayed in my mind. A few minutes later I was sat, Bible open, sipping coffee and found myself drawn to an Old Testament scripture:

"The fire on the altar must be kept burning; it must not go out. Every morning the priest is to add firewood and arrange the burnt offering on the fire and burn the fat of the fellowship offerings on it. The fire must be kept burning on the altar continuously; it must not go out." (Leviticus 6:12-13)

I read and re-read the passage, allowing the command of God to resound in my own spirit. "Fire must be kept burning … it must not go out … every morning … add firewood … the fire must be kept burning continuously … it must not go out!"

This emphatic command was written for Old Testament priests, but today every believer is a priest under the New Covenant (2 Peter 2:9). We too are expected to keep the fire in our hearts burning and growing.

When John Wesley was asked why so many people over so many years kept coming to hear him preach, he simply said, "I set myself on fire and the world comes to watch me burn."

A life of fire is irresistible to those we come into contact with every day. Your heart was created to burn with God's love and presence. Don't settle for anything less than God's best! God's Word, the Bible, is the book we must all feed on every day and, by the inspiration and work of the Holy Spirit, it is the book that sets us on fire. Don't substitute other books for God's book, but allow this devotional to supplement your reading of God's Word.

I would encourage you to take your time over these devotions each day. Begin with prayer, still your mind, and ask the Lord to speak to you and awaken your heart. It is interaction and engagement with Him that transforms us. Be aware of His nearness and desire to meet with you every day.

"..if my fire is not large it is yet real, and there may be those who can light their candle at its flame."
– AW Tozer, *Pursuit of God*

"If Jesus Christ be
God and died for me,
then no sacrifice can
be too great for me to
make for Him."
— C.T. Studd

1

HIGHLY FLAMMABLE

———•———

"Immediately the fire of the Lord flashed down from heaven..."

(1 Kings 18:38 NLT)

———•———

You have a choice about how you live your life. You can live in a cold, apathetic way, just drifting from one day to the next. Or you can know the fiery passion of the love of God burning in your heart. I want to help you to understand how to make your life highly flammable!

Allow me to pull some lessons from a well known Old Testament story. It's a true story, recounting events that actually took place, but as with many stories in Scripture, it also offers us a parable for our own lives.

Elijah the prophet was confronted with gross idolatry in the land. The altar of the Lord was in ruins and the people of God had lost their way. Read the story in 1 Kings chapter 18. Things came to a head and Elijah, full of passion for his God, wanted to show the people a demonstration of God's power. Elijah repaired the altar of the Lord with 12 stones, representing each of the tribes of Israel, arranged a sacrificial offering, and then had the people saturate it with water.

Drenched in water, there was no way the offering was going to set alight, but Elijah called upon the Lord. The "fire of the Lord" fell and consumed *"the sacrifice, the wood, the stones and the soil, and also licked up the water in the trench."*

Let's hear what God has to say to us about our own lives through this story.

Come here to me

Elijah gathered the people around him saying, *"Come here and see what God will do..."*. He wanted them to see God at work in impossible circumstances so that they would be inspired and challenged. In the same way, you and I are called to demonstrate to those close to us what God *can* and *is* doing. In Christ, we are also called to live in close enough proximity to others that they will see how we live our lives, so that it will inspire them to live differently.

I believe the Holy Spirit is at work in the world today, empowering believers to be natural witnesses of Christ. We can impact others simply by how we live, how we demonstrate and represent Jesus to others. As we determine to live in the power of His Spirit we will not only touch the lives of those who don't know Jesus yet, but we will also inspire and motivate others in their walk with Jesus.

Pause for reflection...

• Pause and think about the people you do life with; those closest to you; your extended family and work colleagues. Ask the Holy Spirit to help you live in such a way that the lives of those people are touched by Him. Ask Father God to help you be a *natural witness* for Jesus.

9

2
REPAIRING THE ALTAR

—•—

"He then put the altar back together, for by now it was in ruins ... he built the stones into the altar in honour of God."

(1 Kings 18:30-35 MSG)

—•—

In our story in 1 Kings, powerfully we see Elijah repairing the altar of the Lord, which lay in ruins. As we know, the altar is the place of worship, of sacrifice; the place of meeting with God. It should have been a place that God's people visited regularly, so that their relationship with Him was cultivated and nurtured. Instead it had been neglected and forgotten.

Relationships are built on encounters with others. If people don't spend time together, having regular meetings and conversations, a relationship will become distant and, at best, irrelevant. At worst, it will simply wither and die. If we want to live a highly flammable life, then this means we need to visit regularly the "altar" of encounter with God. If that altar is currently in disrepair, or has been neglected, it's time to rebuild it and guard it jealously.

We know that relationships don't just take care of themselves – we have to be intentional in our pursuit of strong, healthy relationships. Although it has been said many times before, this is why it's good for us to have a time/place where we meet with Father God, every day. A designated time/place, set aside for intimacy. To neglect this is to expose our spiritual lives to danger. During our time with God we receive "fresh bread" from Heaven – new revelation, new insight, spiritual strength…

12 Stones

The stones that Elijah used symbolically in this story spoke of the people's history with God. It spoke of those who had gone before them, reminding them that they were part of a bigger picture. Judges 2:10 speaks of a generation of people who had grown up but *"neither knew the Lord, nor the works He had done for Israel."*

We mustn't forget what God has done in our lives. This verse also reminds us why we need to tell our children the stories of God's goodness from our own lives. We have a spiritual inheritance that needs to be passed on safely to our children and their children. We all need reminders of God's goodness to us. We must purposefully place "stones of remembrance" in our lives – things that will remind and encourage us every time we see them. Print out specific scriptures God has spoken to you that are significant for your life. Record answers to specific prayers in a journal, so you can look back and see God's hand in your life.

Let's be purposeful about meeting with our God and remembering all He has done.

Pause for reflection...

Life is busy, we all know that. But make time with God a priority in your life, however and wherever you choose to do it. If your "altar of encounter" with God is in disrepair, take steps to lovingly rebuild it. God will always welcome you into His presence.

3
WATER AND FIRE

———•———

"All Scripture is God-breathed and is useful for teaching,
rebuking, correcting and training in righteousness, so that
the servant of God may be thoroughly equipped for every
good work."
(2 Timothy 3:16-17 NIV)

———•———

As Elijah laid the stones that rebuilt the altar of the Lord, he was reminding us that we can build our lives on God's goodness and His promises to us, because He is faithful and His Word is rock solid. We can remind ourselves of His past visitations in our lives and His commitment to our future in the place of encounter.

Elijah then prepared a sacrifice to the Lord. What can this mean for us today? If we desire to live a passionate life for Jesus, consumed by His love, then there will be precious things in our life that we may need to lay down. Some of us cling to sinful habits. For others, maybe it is as simple as our priorities going astray. Still others are distracted by "stuff". The truth is, the accumulation of "stuff" in our lives has reached epidemic proportions. Companies sell storage space to people whose houses are too small to store all of their belongings!

Whatever it is that might distract us from our purpose, we need to bring it before God and place it on the altar. What do you need to put on the altar today?

God gives us lots of things to enjoy in life, and many relationships we can cherish, but these things should not consume us to the point that they push God out of His rightful place in our lives, as Lord. We also must not succumb to the subtle trap of allowing the *blessings* of God to replace the *presence* of God in our lives.

When the altar was ready, Elijah poured water over it. The Bible is not explicit, but we assume it was to ensure that what followed could not be interpreted as anything other than a supernatural sign. But the Bible uses the imagery of both fire and water at different times. Water often represents the cleansing power of the Word of God. Those who want to live highly flammable lives will be immersed in His Word, absorbing its truth. God's Word is also like a fire that burns in our hearts. Many miss the power of imbibing the Word of God, meditating on it, drinking it in. But the Word is living and powerful. Soak in the Bible. In fact, overdose on it! Store up its truth and confess it!

When Elijah cried out to the Lord, He answered with fire. Surrender your all to God, lay down everything on His altar, and you will always get fire – heavenly fire!

Pause for reflection...

• It's easy to get wrapped up in our lives to the point where we lose perspective. It's good to take inventory of our lives on a regular basis and examine our priorities.

• Are there things in your life that are eating up all your time and maybe need to be laid on God's altar?

• God's Word is the ultimate leveller. Spend time in the Bible and your priorities will come into alignment as you are washed by the Word.

"Here is the path to the higher life: down, lower down! Just as water always seeks and fills the lowest place, so the moment God finds men abased and empty, His glory and power flow in to exalt and to bless."
–Andrew Murray, Humility

4
DEAD MAN WALKING

"Truly, truly, I say to you, unless a grain of wheat falls into the earth and dies, it remains alone; but if it dies, it bears much fruit."
(John 12:24 ESV)

True Christianity begins with death, which then leads to life. The problem for many today is that we are trying to access the life and power of God without embracing death. This leads to frustration and weakness in believers who end up living powerless lives, constantly struggling to overcome. The power of the Holy Spirit flows through those who have died and now live in the Spirit.

Are you ready to die?

We have to die in order to live by surrendering the whole of our lives to our Father God. There is no escaping this truth. It is threaded throughout Jesus' teaching and the epistles of Paul. Both Jesus and Paul were examples of *dead men walking*. Their lives were utterly surrendered. They had put to death their own agendas, desires and plans in order to live according to the Father's will.

Jesus is our ultimate role model for life and ministry. His earthly life was lived as a surrendered life, to do the will of His Father. Every day of His life was lived on purpose, led by the Father through the Holy Spirit.

Jesus did nothing of Himself or for Himself, but only what He saw the Father doing. We see the ultimate example of this as Jesus is obedient in going to the cross.

I believe today that God is gathering an army of surrendered, "burning ones" to be fruitful, destroying the works of the enemy wherever they go. Men and women who will advance the Kingdom of God by manifesting the life of God in signs, wonders, miracles and salvation. But there is no shortcut. It begins with a surrendered life. The death of our self-life is not to be feared, but willingly embraced. Our heavenly Father is all loving and can be trusted with our lives.

The crux of the matter is this: *are we willing to surrender our will to His will?*

Speaking from experience I can say that it's easier if we surrender willingly and don't try to fight God. The Christians who live frustrated lives are those who try to keep parts of their lives for themselves. Or they surrender things grudgingly, then try to sneak them back. All this does is unnecessarily prolong the dying process!

Reflect on this poignant quote from Smith Wigglesworth – a man to whom God entrusted a remarkable ministry filled with signs and wonders:

> "Before God could bring me to this place
> He has broken me a thousand times."

Instead of having to be broken, let's willingly lay down our lives to God.

Pause for reflection...

• The *natural* part in each of us resists death. We don't like anything we perceive could be painful, so we run from it. But in the *supernatural* economy of the Kingdom, things work in precisely the opposite way. Death to self leads to life. Surrender is the beginning of an incredible, abundant life. The point at which we stop trying to work out our lives for ourselves, and become utterly dependent on God, is the point at which He can begin to fill our lives with purpose and meaning.

• Start a habit of speaking out your surrender to God every morning and pray that He would have control over your circumstances. Trust in His unfailing love for you.

5
PRAY, PRAY, PRAY

————•————

"Look to the LORD and his strength; seek his face always."
(1 Chronicles 16:11 NIV)

————•————

Prayer is a vital part of our relationship with God. Without it, we don't see or experience God's heart for us and for His world. Prayer isn't about ritual, but about friendship. It draws us closer into the compassion of God and sparks faith for the miraculous. The more we pray, the deeper we go and the more we burn for the things God cares about. Prayer is not an add-on to the Christian life, it is the heart of it.

You only need to look at the life of Jesus in the Gospels to see how often He talked to His Father. John 17: 6-26 is a beautiful example of His love and concern for His disciples, expressed as a prayer. We are told to pray without ceasing in 1 Thessalonians 5:17 because that is what God wants – to be in constant communion with us.

Be inspired
George Müller was a German missionary who moved to England in 1829 and began a ministry that spanned almost 70 years. As well as building 5 large orphanages, pastoring a church of 1200 and running a publishing house, he did 3 world preaching tours after the age of 70! To George Müller, prayer was just like breathing. He lived by the conviction that all he had to do was to tell his Heavenly Father what he needed, and all would be well.

There are so many accounts of answered prayer during the life and ministry of this amazing man and at the end of his life, when asked how he managed to see such miraculous fruitfulness he said:

"There was a day when I died; died to self, my opinions, preferences, tastes and will; died to the world, its approval or censure; died to the approval or blame even of my brethren or friends; and since then I have studied only to show myself approved unto God."

Let's be like George Müller.

I want to encourage you to take some time to reflect and talk to the Lord about what He wants you to do. If you are serious about becoming one of God's *burning ones*, there is a cost involved. There is no half-hearted surrender. If we are to see more of the miraculous power of God in these days, a life of prayer is the only way.

Pause for reflection...

• Prayer is the oxygen of the Christian life. It is as essential as your next breath. But prayer needn't be a religious ritual. Rather it's a conversation with our Father; an ongoing dialogue that nurtures and feeds our relationship with Him. Let's emulate George Müller and make prayer and the presence of God our top priority.

"I desire many things concerning myself; but I desire nothing so much, as to have a heart filled with love to the Lord. I long for a warm personal attachment to Him." –George Müller

6
ONE MAGNIFICENT OBSESSION

"Jesus looked at them and said, 'With man this is impossible,
but with God all things are possible.'"
(Matthew 19:26 ESV)

One of the great hallmarks of highly flammable people is their absolute love for and devotion to Jesus. This devotion will eclipse all other loves in their lives. Because of it, people will see the power of the Holy Spirit manifest through them every day.

I want to invite you to imagine how that would look in your life. Think about the situations you want to see God change for the better. Let me remind you how Jesus' close relationship with His Heavenly Father opened the way for the presence of God to come and heal the sick. Remember that He reassured us that we would do greater things than He did (John 14:12).

God is awakening people so that their relationship with Him is not reduced to a formula or a prayer, but is a living, dynamic reality with substance. I believe that it is on God's heart to pour out more and more of His Holy Spirit, resulting in unprecedented signs and wonders.

There is a challenge we need to overcome if we are to see this, however. I believe that traditions of men and dry, man-made theology has sucked the life out of the joy of the Gospel. We are used to living with a watered-down version of Christianity that has nothing to do with the Kingdom of God.

What's stopping you?

A hallmark of this watered-down Christian life is a low expectation when it comes to prayer.

We have all faced the pain of disappointment and prayers that seem to have been unanswered. Sometimes, this can leave us reluctant to step out and pray for the same things the next time. In the same way, a theology which preaches the "Gospel" but leaves out Jesus, means that we never really have permission to have faith in His finished work.

We mustn't settle for second best with Jesus. A magnificent obsession requires us to lay down our disappointments, fears and regrets at the foot of the cross and allow the Holy Spirit to change our perspective, so that we lift our eyes to see all He is and all He does. God wants to help you reconnect with truth and He is after your heart.

Instead of settling for a small God, let's say with the hymn writer:

My hope is built on nothing less
Than Jesus' blood and righteousness.
I dare not trust the sweetest frame,
But wholly trust in Jesus' Name.
-*Edward Mote*

Pause for reflection...

• The "normal" Christian life is one filled with the dynamic activity of the Holy Spirit. If this has not been your experience, it's time to raise your expectations, because God is at work today and He wants to use you! Pray and expect to see more of God's power in your life today.

7
THE GREATEST ADVENTURE

———•———

"For we are His workmanship, created in Christ Jesus for good works, which God prepared beforehand that we should walk in them."
(Ephesians 2:10 NKJV)

———•———

Once we have come into relationship with the Father through the Son, by the power of the Holy Spirit, our adventure begins. It requires us to become a radical disciple; unafraid to be changed by the Lord, learning from the Master and submitting to Him in every area of our life.

Imagine for a moment you were about to embark on a long trek through deep jungle. It would certainly require stamina, preparation and commitment, and you would doubtless have a mixture of emotions as you thought about what lay ahead. Unfamiliar territory, varied weather, possible dangers and incredible beauty face you. It would be foolish and reckless to go alone, so you would want an experienced guide who could protect and lead you through all that was ahead.

God never leaves us alone as we start our greatest adventure of a relationship with Him. It is wonderful to know He can be trusted to lead us and guide us through life's journey, and it is our responsibility to submit to Him and His expertise. We need to obey Him, do what He shows us to do, listen as He shows us the way, and trust that He will enable us and empower us to do it all.

Always with us

When we have the promise of the presence of Jesus with us always, we can live lives that are hallmarked by dynamic fruitfulness and power. Many live mediocre lives and go through unnecessary battles because they have failed to see that submitting totally to Jesus is the better way. How easy it is to get lost that way. I've said it before, but complete surrender and trust is the only way to live the greatest adventure in life. Jesus' lordship must touch our relationships, money, ambitions, careers, leisure time and everything else.

But the wonderful promise we have in return is that He will never leave us or forsake us. We are intimately known to Him and He knows what is best for us. He hears our prayers and our dreams and, in return for our complete abandonment to Him, He will lead and guide us through a life that will be so much more exciting and fulfilling than we could ever imagine.

Let's reject fear and a life of mediocrity and embrace the adventure to come, with Jesus at our side.

Pause for reflection...

• Reflect on the truth that no matter what life throws at you, God has promised that He will never leave you or forsake you. The truth is, God is more committed to our wellbeing, spiritual welfare, and material provision than we are ourselves. We are His!

• The entire Christian life is a journey of learning to trust God more and more. When we trust Him wholeheartedly, life is an ever-deepening adventure.

"We must cease striving and trust God to provide what He thinks is best and in whatever time He chooses to make it available. But this kind of trusting doesn't come naturally. It's a spiritual crisis of the will in which we must choose to exercise faith."
–Charles R. Swindoll

8
JESUS – THE HEAD AND THE HEART

———•———

"I know all the things you do. I have seen your hard work
and your patient endurance ... But ... You don't love me or
each other as you did at first! ... Turn back to me..."
(Revelation 2:2-5 NLT)

———•———

There is no point giving Jesus the lordship over our lives,
families, ministries and churches unless we also allow Him to
be the heart of everything. The balance of the *authority* and the
love of Jesus is a perfect one. The Christian life is not a buffet
meal from which we pick and choose as we like. It is an all-
consuming relationship with the Creator of the universe, made
possible by His Son's death.

What does this mean for us?

We must remember to hold these two things in tension.
There will be times when we experience His lavish love and
times when, as the Head of all things, we will know His rebuke.
As an encouragement, let me remind you that love is at the
core of the Christian Gospel, so any rebuke will never be harsh
or cruel. But it does mean that sometimes we need to be told
when things are not quite right.

In the book of Revelation, the church at Ephesus was
commended for doing a lot of things well, including being
hard workers and enduring much hardship in the name of
Jesus. However, good deeds alone were not enough for Jesus.
The church was rebuked for missing something important that
they could not function without. Put simply, they had forsaken

their first love. Read about it in Revelation 2:2-5.

All their activity and good church management paled into insignificance compared to their neglect of their love for Jesus. It is an issue that God takes very seriously indeed and the Head of the Church had something strong to say about it.

Keep the love burning

We mustn't forget what first drew us into a relationship with Jesus. That moment when we were blown away by a revelation of just how loved we are should always be protected. It should form the foundation of every part of our lives. Like the Ephesians, I believe in working hard, but never at the cost of losing my first love. It is Jesus who gives meaning to all our activity and we need to burn with passion for Him alone.

Pause for reflection...

• Meditate on the truth that God is not a taskmaster who wants us to perform for Him, but a Lover who wants us to be immersed in the joy of knowing Him deeply.

• Simply loving Jesus and focusing our attention on Him should be our top priority. All worthwhile activity flows from this.

9
ALL CHANGE

———•———

This same Good News ... is bearing fruit everywhere by changing lives, just as it changed your lives from the day you first heard and understood the truth about God's wonderful grace."
(Colossians 1:6 NLT)

———•———

Our dynamic love relationship with Jesus will change us to become just like Him. The journey of faith doesn't end with salvation; it has only just begun. God has destined us to be conformed to the likeness of Jesus. Rather than leave us as He found us, He takes time to lovingly reshape us, so that we reflect His beautiful image.

Think of it this way: when we live and grow up in a family unit, our way of seeing the world is influenced by our relationships within it. Our personality and character is fashioned over many years of interactions with the group of people we grow up alongside. There will inevitably be times of shared joy, sorrow, conflict, irritation, encouragement and so on. All of this makes us who we are to some degree, and helps us become independent human beings.

But God wants to take us further!

Here's the good news

The wonderful thing about belonging to God is that whatever our experiences of family life, positive or negative, God is committed to transforming us into *His* family likeness. This means He enhances the positives and transforms the negatives, so we can be free to manifest His power in a greater way. God knows what we have been through, and nothing is too difficult for Him to reshape. He wants to set you free so that greater fruitfulness will be evident in your life.

Do you want to burn with passion for Jesus? Do you want to make the devil afraid? Then give God permission to change you. The more like Jesus you become, the more dangerous you are to the domain of darkness. It is Christ in you, the hope of glory that is the power source (Colossians 1:27).

Change is never easy. Today's Church has believed a lie that God's primary purpose is to bless them or make their lives easier. This is not true. God is more concerned about forming the likeness of His Son in you than giving you a comfortable life.

Are you ready for change? You can trust your loving Father to lead the process as you submit to Him. Reflect on this powerful quote from Francis Frangipane:

"What pleases the Father most is not what proceeds from our hands, but what rises from our hearts. He is seeking the revelation of His Son in us."

Pause for reflection...

• Take time to think about some of the character traits you've grown up with, that have been influenced by your family. Some will be positive while others, perhaps, may be negative. But whether good or bad, God wants us to be transformed by taking on His family characteristics. Galatians 5:22-23 spells them out. The more we are filled with the Holy Spirit, the more we will reflect them.

"The best use of life is love. The best expression of love is time. The best time to love is now."
–Rick Warren

10
LIKE JESUS IN CHARACTER AND POWER

———·———

*"Let love be your highest goal! But you should also desire the
special abilities the Spirit gives..."*
(1 Corinthians 14:1 NLT)

———·———

To become more like Jesus, we must understand that power
and character go hand in hand. In John 14:12 we see that we
need to imitate Jesus by moving in power like He did. In John
13:15 it is the character of Jesus that we are told to set as our
example. I want you to read these verses and allow the truth
contained in them to bring light to you today. Let the Holy
Spirit encourage you and begin to imagine how different your
life will be when you make these two things your goal.

Please know that they are not optional extras. We are called
to immerse ourselves in the nature and character of God.
Some try to hide behind the gifts of the Spirit and think that
because they operate in them, they are exempt from having
their character shaped by God. Others think that because they
function well in the fruits of the Spirit, that they are excused
from manifesting His power.

We need both to get the job done.

Not left as orphans
If Jesus had ascended into heaven and that was it, there would
be no way we could live lives as His highly flammable followers.
It would all have been over very quickly. Instead, in John 14,
He tells His disciples to expect something very special. They

were not going to be left all alone, as orphans, but be given access to God in an incredible way. The power was to come not from human effort or good works, but from His Holy Spirit who would impart the very life of Christ into every part of them.

The Holy Spirit is a key person, as it is He who forms the likeness of Christ in us. He is both the giver of the gifts (1 Corinthians 12:7-11) and the grower of fruit in our lives (Galatians 5:22-25). Without the Holy Spirit, we would never be like Jesus in character or in power, but with Him it is His nature that manifests through our flesh and blood.

Do you want your life to be guided by truth? Do you want to live as Jesus lived? Ask God to fill you with His Spirit. We must resist sin and submit to God and His ways. Take time to meditate on the life and ministry of Jesus and let hope and faith rise in you today.

Pause for reflection...

• Jesus' gift to His first followers is available for all His followers for all time. We have the same access to God's power through the Holy Spirit dwelling in us. This means we can live supernaturally natural lives. Being filled with the Spirit is an ongoing process, so pray now that God would fill you afresh.

11
FACE TO FACE

———•———

"You will show me the way of life, granting me the joy of your presence and the pleasures of living with you forever.
(Psalm 16:11 NLT)

———•———

Have you ever experienced that moment when you hold a baby in your arms and before you know it, you are aware of the most wonderful smile coming at you? And babies don't just smile with their mouths, they smile with their eyes, which somehow speaks of the presence of a deep soul in that tiny bundle.

Jesus wants us to look at Him that way. The Bible tells us that when we do, we reflect the glory of God and it transforms us into His likeness. (See 2 Corinthians 3:16-18)

I have said for years that whatever you look at, you become like. Many Christians are depressed, confused and anxious because they spend too much time looking at negative images. Although social media has many positive uses, it is also awash with negative propaganda and unhelpful images that can hijack our peace. Negative images dull people's senses and they can absorb confusion, violence and sorrow into their hearts, wondering why they can't access joy. They carry a burden of foreboding when God wants them to walk in the light and be overcomers.

Switch it off
It's time to reject the world and its message of gloom and destruction. Jesus knew we would experience troubles in life,

but He encouraged us to not be afraid (John 14:27). It's time to stop indulging in looking at images that bring sadness, fear and anger, and begin to turn our faces to Jesus, where we will find only love and peace. Change what you look at if you want to be set on fire for God! Open your Bible more and allow its deep truths to sink into your heart. Spend time worshipping God and look at His face.

I believe it is impossible to be a burning Jesus-follower if there isn't the commitment and sacrifice to pursuing His presence. This quote from my friend Bob Sorge says it so well:

> "When you're in His presence for extended periods, the molecular composition of your soul gets restructured. You start to think differently, and you don't even know why. You start to have different passions and interests, and you don't even know why ... the secret is simply this: take large chunks of time in God's presence."

Focus your attention on Jesus' face and look for His smile of affirmation. Spend time close to Him in worship, reading the Word and in prayer. You can do this on your own or with others, it doesn't matter. It just matters that you do it.

Pause for reflection...

• Take an honest look at a snapshot of your life – say one week. How much time do you spend looking at things that don't add anything to your spiritual life? (Social media is an easy target, but there are many other distractions!) Let's decide to spend more time "looking" towards God instead. As you shift your focus, you'll find your heart being transformed by His grace.

"Continue seeking God with seriousness.
Unless He wanted you, you would not be
wanting Him."
—C.S. Lewis

NEVER WASTE A GOOD TRIAL

*"I, your God, have a firm grip on you and I'm not letting go.
I'm telling you, 'Don't panic. I'm right here to help you.'"*
(Isaiah 41:13 MSG)

True surrender to Jesus will mean that life is not always easy. In fact, we will probably experience times of trial that will, on occasion, push us to the limit of our human resources. We may feel "got at" or alone in our struggle, and feel that no one understands. We may wonder if God has abandoned us or feel like the enemy has the upper hand.

Think for a moment about the last time you had one of these trials. You may be going through one now. What is your view of God? Are you angry with Him or disappointed that He has not delivered you from your suffering? You may not feel Him close to you right now, but I want to encourage you that it doesn't mean He has left you. In fact, the opposite is true.

Working together for the good

Romans 8:28 tells us that God works everything out for the good. The following verse talks about being conformed to the image of Christ by all things, good and bad. We can therefore be reassured that God uses people and situations to change us, and there is no accident or chance in the circumstances of our lives or the people we encounter.

So instead of gritting your teeth and waiting for a trial to pass so you can experience blessing, ask yourself the question:

"Lord, what do you want to teach me through this problem?" Once you begin to think like that, it will change your perspective and lift your eyes to Jesus and away from yourself. It will draw you away from the issue and into a place of worship.

We are all made in the image of God, but we can also be self-centred. If trials make us bitter or entitled, we lose God's precious gifts of grace and mercy to see us through.

Smith Wigglesworth went through many trials, but he could still say this:

"We have such a lovely Jesus. He always proves Himself to be such a mighty Deliverer. He never fails to plan the best things for us."

Can we say the same when we're in the middle of a hard time? When pressure is applied on you, what comes out? Meditate on the truth that trials are opportunities to deepen our trust in Jesus and let the light of the Holy Spirit shine from within.

Pause for reflection...

• When trials come our way, it's very tempting to look inwards and retreat, or to look outwards for someone or somethng to blame. Instead we need to look upwards. To once again put our focus on Jesus.

• If you're going through a tough time at present, I implore you to put that trial in Jesus' hands, entrust it to Him, and wait and see what He will do. He won't let you down.

13
TRANSFORMATION TIME

"I'll pour pure water over you and scrub you clean. I'll give you a new heart, put a new spirit in you. I'll remove the stone heart from your body and replace it with a heart that's God-willed, not self-willed."
(Ezekiel 36:26 MSG)

Becoming more and more like Jesus is the aim of every burning believer. The New Testament word for "transformation" is *metamorphoo* – meaning to change into another form. It is the root of our word "metamorphosis", which describes what happens when a caterpillar becomes a butterfly or a tadpole becomes a frog. There is a complete change.

God does not rush this process of transformation. He takes His time with us and we change little by little. If we are to live highly flammable lives, God desires that every part of us is changed forever. No longer will we be pushed around by the enemy or give way to the lusts of the flesh. Full transformation requires us to submit to a deep work of God, so that we have no desire to be drawn away from His rest and presence.

In the cocoon
When a butterfly is forming in the cocoon, very little evidence of what is happening is visible from the outside. All the work of death and regeneration is happening on the inside, until the day of breakout finally arrives. In the same way, God will invite us to hide in Him while the Holy Spirit brings the change

within. He knows what needs to die in us to make room for His Holy Spirit's power.

If you feel hidden away at the moment and have become frustrated you are not seeing more of God's power, don't be discouraged. If you have submitted to Jesus, I guarantee change is happening right now!

The new generation of Jesus-followers who are arising on the earth will be powerful, unstoppable and known in heaven and hell. It will be their Christlikeness that will make them dangerous and contagious, just like Jesus modelled when He walked on earth.

I believe that we are not always sure what it is inside us that needs God's transforming touch. I think this is a good thing. If we knew ourselves as well as, or better than, God, there would be no sacrifice or trust and only partial change. It is vital we let the Holy Spirit do His work in us. No transformation process is the same as another. You are unique and God's gentle but strong power is complete and perfect, just for you.

Let's be committed to submitting to His perfect will for our lives.

Pause for reflection...

• Though you may not realise it, God is at work in you right now, by His Spirit, working towards your transformation. Make it your aim today to cooperate with the work God is doing in the secret place of your heart.

"A drowning man cannot be saved until he is utterly exhausted and ceases to make the slightest effort to save himself."
–Watchman Nee

14

KEEP THE FLAME BURNING

———•———

"Don't burn out; keep yourselves fuelled and aflame. Be alert
servants of the Master, cheerfully expectant. Don't quit in
hard times; pray all the harder. Help needy Christians; be
inventive in hospitality."
(Romans 12:11-13 MSG)

———•———

We have a responsibility to live continually in the presence of
God. How easy it is to revel in those special encounters with
the Lord when His Holy Spirit burns within and hope fills our
hearts. Everything looks and feels different and we imagine
changing the world in an instant. But in a few days, we find
ourselves back to the daily grind and, as the flame dies, we
believe the lie that it is normal to live "in and out" of these
experiences. They become a special treat, reserved only for
conferences or other events.

It is time to overcome this deception. We are created to
live continually in that place of overcoming faith and buoyant
hope, expressing itself through lavish love.

When we fall in love with a person, we want to be with them
all the time. Dreams of a future together dominate our thoughts
and our hearts beat with love, passion, joy and excitement.
But any human relationship, like a fire, if left unattended,
will eventually burn out and go cold. It is just as true in our
relationship with Jesus. I have had to contend with this on my
own walk with God and I have counselled many others in the

same place. They describe their passion for Jesus in the past tense and wonder what happened.

Fuel for the journey

An initial encounter with God isn't enough to fuel an individual for the rest of his or her life. We are not meant to splutter to a standstill before the finish line on a reserve tank, but be constantly filled with the "fuel" of the Holy Spirit through to eternity.

If you can identify with this scenario, it's time for action. Perhaps life has treated you in such a way that disappointments and distractions have shifted everything down a gear? Perhaps you have run out of fuel and are at a standstill? The truth is that God has called you to a life of radical, fiery power for the long haul and it is time now to humbly repent and ask to be filled with power every day.

Let's meditate on the words of Jesus, our ultimate example:

"I tell you the truth, the Son can do nothing by himself; he can do only what he sees his Father doing, because whatever the Father does, the Son also does." (John 5:19)

Pause for reflection...

• Reflect on the truth that God wants to meet with you continually, not just on special occasions. He desires to walk with you in every aspect of your life; to fill the ordinary situations of life with His supernatural presence.
• Perhaps it's time to re-ignite your faith by doing something different? Form a prayer triplet with a couple of friends, meet regularly, and challenge each other to go deeper with God.

"I want the presence of God Himself, or I don't want anything at all to do with religion... I want all that God has or I don't want any."
—A.W. Tozer

15
ALONE BUT NOT LONELY

"Be still, and know that I am God!"
(Psalm 46:10 NLT)

Jesus' life and ministry was marked by passion and obedience. Everything He did flowed from a living, intimate and intense relationship with His Heavenly Father. He speaks about it in John 5:30, acknowledging that He could do nothing in Himself, because everything came from the will of God and not His own plans. Jesus knew that without this intimacy, He would become distracted from His call and purpose. It was the bedrock of everything.

I sometimes wonder how Jesus coped with all the crowds and all the demands on His time. It is true that He had plenty of persecution and trouble; rejected almost daily, misunderstood by the religious leaders of the day and left alone by His friends (John 6:66). But through it all, Jesus remained close to His Father and often left the mayhem to find a place to be alone to pray (Mark 1:35).

Time out

Life is often very busy. We fill our diaries with so many appointments and events that it can be difficult to carve out time to breathe and just be alone with God. It's possible, too, that we find we take value and affirmation from being over busy, whilst inside we are aching for that deep connection with our Heavenly Father.

Don't be afraid to be alone. Solitude is not the same as isolation. Remember that the devil will do all he possibly can to prevent your relationship with God from growing and deepening. He does not want you to burn with passion for Jesus, he wants you to be mediocre at best and discouraged and disappointed at worst. Yet all the time, God is waiting to spend time with you. He isn't calling you to crushing loneliness, but intimate *aloneness* with Him. Of course, we need human relationships to enrich our lives, but not at the cost of the most important relationship of all.

Let's fill our time wisely. Balance the diary a bit better so that you become more disciplined in finding times of solitude with God. Jesus often did this in the morning, but He did it at other times too, so find your rhythm and see how it changes you. A burning life of miracles with passion and commitment cannot happen in the flesh, it happens in the Spirit, and it will only happen when we submit to the will of our Father, just as Jesus did.

Pause for reflection...

• When was the last time you were truly alone with God. No one around; phone turned off; no distractions; just you and Father God. When we're alone it can take a bit of time to turn off the "background noise" of life. But when we reach that place of real stillness before God, He nearly always speaks into the silence.

16
THE DAILY RELATIONAL ENCOUNTER

—.—

"And after he had dismissed the crowds, he went up on the mountain by himself to pray. When evening came, he was there alone..."

(Matthew 14:23 NLT)

—.—

In the next few readings, we will explore together how we can have a daily relational encounter with our Heavenly Father. The goal for these times with God is not so we can tick off a "quiet time" rota as part of a religious exercise. Instead, we will pursue the presence of God and grow in depth and intimacy. It is relationship that matters, not ritual. If your times with God have become all about going through a programme of reading and even praying which leave you unchanged, but make you feel like you've done the right thing, then it's no surprise nothing changes. Religious duty will never satisfy the deep longing of the human heart. In fact, it can often be a shroud that disguises the ugliness of sin and the chains of unforgiveness.

Jesus knows when this is happening. Read His words in Matthew 15:8:

"These people honour me with their lips but their hearts are from me."

It is the power of God we need to help us overcome. This power forgives sin, heals the sick and destroys the works of the evil one. This power cannot come from religious observance; it must come from intimacy.

Change is on its way

Every time we meet with God, we are changed. It is vital we expect this. So many of us will have grown up to do the right thing and have a quiet time because this was part of being a Christian. I was led to believe growing up that most of my quiet times would be dry and boring! How grateful I am that I have since learned that if I approach the Father relationally with faith, then every encounter can be a life-transforming one.

Let's be intentional now. Make these encounters a daily occurrence by going to the same place of quiet and solitude. Turn off your gadgets and prepare your heart for a meeting with the One who waits for you and who loves your soul. He has things to say to you, and He has ideas to share with you. He may put His finger on something in you that needs to change, but He will do it lovingly and with grace. He is also an exceptional listener and can be completely trusted, so be free to pour out your heart and let His presence fill you.

Let's get started.

Pause for reflection...

• When we make time to be silent before God, He will speak into our hearts. If you can, make a habit of writing down whatever God speaks to you. It's amazing to look back and read what God has said and how often He has spoken to us.

17

ENCOUNTERING GOD: HEART TO HEART

—·—

"And the peace of God, which surpasses all understanding,
will guard your hearts and your minds in Christ Jesus."
(Philippians 4:7 NLT)

—·—

I teach that there are five simple ingredients to a fruitful daily encounter with God.

The first is about the *connection of the heart*. God is a relational Being. Not only is relationship at the centre of who He is in the Trinity, but He made us in His image so that we would know His love and give our love in return. When we take time out with Him, it is less about what we do and more about what we expect. We should anticipate that God wants a two-way connection with us in the same way we would cultivate a human relationship.

Every relationship needs to be nurtured. There is no benefit in being married and keeping the conversation shallow or never spending intimate, quality time together. In fact, that can be a recipe for disaster. When feelings, desires, hopes and dreams are left unshared, a wide canyon opens between the couple which is virtually impossible to cross. It is then that distractions can appear and the relationship becomes vulnerable.

However, when a couple choose to be fully present and give their complete attention to one another, the bond deepens, strengthens and intimacy grows.

So, what do I do?

I often start my time with the Lord by simply telling Him I am ready and waiting to meet with Him. I thank Him that He loves me and that He is ready to meet with me too. I ask Him to open my eyes, my ears and my heart so I can see Him, hear Him and love Him in return. I tell Him there is nothing more precious to me than His presence and nothing more important than His glory.

You will see that this is about as far from religious ritual as it is possible to get. Keep it simple. Don't waste words or fall into the trap of petitioning God for things you need. There will be time for that later. You are approaching the King of Kings and Lord of Lords who is also your Father and loves you enough to send His son to die for you. If ever there is a quality heart to heart connection it is this one, so give yourself completely to it and be filled with wonder that, through Jesus, you have access to a love relationship like no other.

Pause for reflection...

• It's easy to come to God with a long shopping list of needs. God loves to meet our needs, but He's not a heavenly vending machine! Instead, come to Him with a list of everything we are thankful for and use it in worshipping Him. When we do this, He often takes care of our needs without us even asking.

"I used to ask God to help me. Then I asked
if I might help Him. I ended up by asking
Him to do His work through me."
                                   –Hudson Taylor

18
ENCOUNTERING GOD: FACE TO FACE

"Seek the Lord and his strength;
seek his presence continually!"
(1 Chronicles 16:11 ESV)

The second ingredient for a fruitful daily encounter with God is a *face to face connection*.

One of the most effective ways to build a relationship with a person is to engage in eye contact. To do that, we obviously need to look at them face to face. So much information can be gathered by watching a person's expressions as they talk; how often they smile and whether they hold a gaze or not. As time goes on, the intimacy deepens and the person's face becomes more familiar to us.

Face to face meetings require a certain level of vulnerability because there is risk involved. The other person may abuse or hurt us, but without ongoing trust and openness, the relationship is doomed to stay superficial. The wonderful thing about God is that you can trust Him with your heart and give Him access to every disappointment, dream and regret.

Meeting with God is a two-way conversation. He won't stay silent because He is a relational Father who loves to talk as well as listen. His presence sits with you and He looks into your eyes, ready to forgive, heal and restore. If you are used to prayer times where you do all the talking, say "Amen", then walk away to get on with your day, that is not an intimate, face to face relationship. To become more like Jesus, we need a deep connection.

So, what do I do?

As you come before the Lord, say, "I'm yours Lord. I'm happy that I can meet with you. I want to surrender myself to you and hold nothing back. I want to look into your face and let you see mine so you can freely roam though me and change me to be more like you."

I want to encourage you to not hide your face from God. It doesn't matter who you are, how you feel or what you have done. The Bible tells us we can draw near to God and He will draw near to us (James 4:8). If we allow our shame or pain to dictate how we approach our Heavenly Father, we are putting our experiences above His goodness. Nothing is too difficult for God to change for the better, so lift your eyes and be bold. It is His face you should seek above all others (Psalm 27:8).

Pause for reflection...

• God's grace towards us is incredible. You may have a lot of guilt and shame over things you've done in your life which you're not proud of. But God doesn't allow those things to disqualify us from receiving His grace and mercy. Come face to face with God today. Tell Him your deepest fears and regrets, and trust Him to heal and restore you.

19
ENCOUNTERING GOD: WORD TO WORD

"For the word of God is living and active, sharper than any two-edged sword, piercing to the division of soul and of spirit, of joints and of marrow, and discerning the thoughts and intentions of the heart."
(Hebrews 4:12 ESV)

The Bible is the written Word of God. It is active, alive and powerful, revealing God's will and purpose. It should be treasured and we should remember how many people have been persecuted or killed for translating or transporting it over the centuries.

Do you love your Bible? Does it nourish you? For those of us who long for a life that burns, the Word of God is essential. It is food for our souls and peace for our minds. It is bursting with truth and alive with fire. It is a mistake to substitute the Bible with any other book, including devotional readings! The Word of God is living, active and sharp (Hebrews 4:12) and we need to be reading it every day in significant amounts.

Imagine a diet that contained only vitamin supplements and no actual food. Not only would your stomach be empty, but you would have decreased energy and be vulnerable to sickness. We need a balanced diet which is substantial. Our body needs this to function in the correct way if we are to remain healthy. Let's remember this as we look for the next devotional offering to hit the shelves. These books are a useful supplement, but they should never be a replacement for the nourishment contained within the Word of God.

So, what do I do?

I want to encourage you to commit to reading the entire Bible through every year. There are many Bible reading plans available online or in your Bible itself. Doing this will immerse you in truth and take you on a journey that sweeps through time. Not only that, but it will lead you into a life of devotion as God illuminates particular passages which meet you where you are, day by day. This will then cause faith to rise in you as you feed on the truth embedded in the words.

Remember that your reading of the Bible is not what impresses God. It is how you allow it to build strength, wisdom, grace and love, so reflecting Jesus, which is what matters to Him most. Ask Him to help you to understand it. Stop as you are reading and pray over the things that challenge or awaken you. God will meet you as you do and your passion will begin to burn in a new way.

Pause for reflection...

• I'm continually amazed by how God can speak into specific situations in our lives using His Word, quickened by the Holy Spirit. Be purposeful in your reading of the Bible, asking God to speak to you, and to speak into specific challenges you are facing in your life.

20
ENCOUNTERING GOD: VOICE TO VOICE

"Pray in the Spirit at all times and on every occasion. Stay alert and be persistent in your prayers for all believers everywhere."
(Ephesians 6:18 NLT)

The fourth ingredient for a fruitful daily encounter with God is a *voice to voice connection*.

Our relationship with God is two-way: when He speaks, we speak back and vice versa. This usually happens as prayer which contains praise, worship, petition, thanksgiving and repentance. Many people have come up with formulas to make prayer more organised, but I don't see it that way. Prayer is relational and is better seen as a conversation than a monologue.

We mustn't forget to listen as well as talk when we pray. You and I have a voice, but so does God. Set time aside to be still and hear what He is saying. He may speak through His Word, bring a thought to mind, speak through a set of circumstances, or give you a dream or vision.

Let me also mention the value of praying in tongues. Jude tells us that we build ourselves up by praying in the Spirit (Jude 20). The more we do it, the more natural it will become, so enabling us to talk to God even when we don't know what to pray in our own language.

So, what do I do?

If your prayer life has become dry, or you need to go to the next level of intimacy with God, the good news is that you can begin by going back to basics.

What are the basics?

I believe they are praise, worship and thanks. Start by thanking God for who He is and all He has done. Imagine telling Him about all the good things you have experienced in your last few weeks and give God the honour for each of those things. The Bible tells us that every good and perfect thing comes from above (James 1:17) so take time to acknowledge God as the source of all good gifts. You will find your soul and spirit begin to stir as you do. This will then flow naturally and gently into a time of petition, confession and repentance.

Finally, be bold in your prayer life! The Bible tells us to approach the throne of God with confidence so that we will be given mercy and grace in our times of need (Hebrews 4:16). I want to encourage you to step away from a timid and meek prayer life and become a warrior who recognises God's beautiful voice above any other.

Pause for reflection...

• Corrie ten Boom asked, "Is prayer your steering wheel or your spare tyre?" For some, prayer is a last resort, but it should always be our first. In prayer, don't worry about the quality of your words, but the quality of your heart. God sees beyond our stumbling attempts at eloquence and instead tunes into the cry of our heart. Make sure that you give time each day for a voice to voice connection with God.

21
ENCOUNTERING GOD: PAGE TO PAGE

"Such things were written in the Scriptures long ago to teach us. And the Scriptures give us hope and encouragement as we wait patiently for God's promises to be fulfilled."

(Romans 15:4 NLT)

The discipline of keeping a spiritual journal is a good one, and it is the fifth ingredient in my toolkit for a fruitful daily encounter with God. As we write down the things the Lord is saying to us, then page by page we have a testimony of His presence in our lives.

How often we forget what God says to us! One of the enemy's strategies is to make us over-busy, so our minds become full of *doing* instead of *being*. Writing down details of the encounters we have with God means that we carry a record of His faithfulness and His love. Our relationship with Him is not just about the things we can remember, but is also about the things we record.

George Müller would do this, calling it "the most profitable plan to meditate with my pen in my hand". It should never become an idol, and we should be able to meet God without doing it, but the simple discipline of writing something down helps impress upon us what God is saying in a deeper way.

In the book of Malachi, we read how those who feared the Lord sat together in His presence and wrote a scroll of remembrance concerning the people who honoured God (Malachi 3:16). This precedent has been kept through the generations and is no less effective today.

ENCOUNTERING GOD: PAGE TO PAGE

So, what do I do?

If it is done with the right heart and attitude, journalling will become something you look forward to doing. We all know what is important to us and how good it is when God speaks to us. No two journals will be alike, because every walk and every encounter with our Heavenly Father will be unique. One of the most important things to write down is when we list the answers to prayers we have prayed. This builds faith and fans the flame of passion for more of God. Likewise, any prophecies you receive should be recorded as they may be fulfilled immediately or take years to bear fruit. Referring to them reveals God's faithfulness and care over all our years.

It doesn't matter how you do it. I have used paper and digital journals and you may want to experiment with both before making up your mind.

Whichever you choose, be purposeful in it as part of your encounter with the Lord.

Pause for reflection...

• Why not take a notebook now and write down some of the significant things God has spoken to you over your life? If this is a brand new concept to you, then ask God to speak to you today, be attentive for His voice, and write down any thoughts or impression that come to you, or any Bible verses that He directs you to. At first you may feel as though you're making up things yourself. This is normal. But as you continue this practice, you will find that the words come from the Holy Spirit and you begin to record things you would never have come up with yourself.

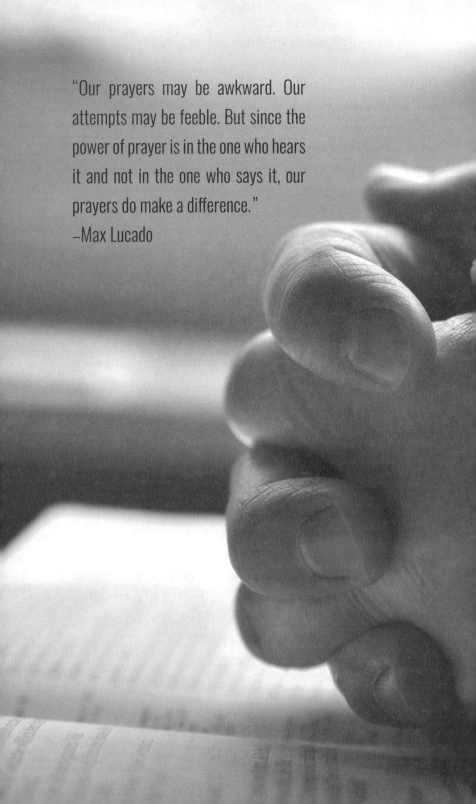

"Our prayers may be awkward. Our attempts may be feeble. But since the power of prayer is in the one who hears it and not in the one who says it, our prayers do make a difference."
–Max Lucado

22
FIRE QUENCHERS

—•—

"Create in me a pure heart, O God,
and renew a steadfast spirit within me."
(Psalm 51:10 NIV)

—•—

While it is important we learn about how to cultivate our relationship with Jesus and kindle the inner flame, it is also necessary to look briefly at those things which can extinguish the fire. There are attitudes and habits we can adopt which grieve the Holy Spirit and they must be avoided at all cost if we are to burn with His holiness.

If you think your human nature will disappear the moment you commit to Jesus, you are mistaken. We all have aspects of our personality and character which, when left unchecked, will seek to dominate our lives. We must not let this happen. The Bible commands us to, *"Above all else, guard your heart, for it is the wellspring of life."* (Proverbs 4:23)

Devotion to Jesus means we must allow our sinful nature to be changed so that we become more and more like Him. The model we have from Jesus is a wonderful one. We see how He always gave His Father the glory (John 8:54), refusing to give way to pride and conceit. We see how He forgave those who had hounded Him to an horrific death on the cross (Luke 23:34) where the burden of injustice and pain must have been overwhelming. If you want to know how to stay clean and on fire, read the gospels again and learn from His example. You will find none better.

Protect your heart

Over the next few readings, we will look in more detail at some specific fire quenchers. When you think about protecting your heart, what does it mean for you? Perhaps you have an issue with pride and enjoy being the centre of attention? Maybe you struggle to forgive people who have wounded you and your heart has become hard? This can lead to isolation and an unwillingness to let people in. Or maybe you struggle with the "spirit of the age" and find it impossible to turn your face away from unhelpful images and idols?

Let me encourage you. God does not condemn or reject you because you have battles. We all have things which can extinguish the flame at times, and the enemy knows how to discourage us as a result. But we have choices to make.

Let's consider how to make good choices to guard our hearts as we read on.

Pause for reflection...

• The psalmist scribed God's words, saying, *"My son, give me your heart and let your eyes delight in my ways."* Think about how your eyes and heart are connected. Protect your inner spiritual life by being vigilant over what you allow your eyes to see.

23
FIRE QUENCHERS: PRIDE

"Do nothing out of selfish ambition or vain conceit. Rather, in humility value others above yourselves."
(Philippians 2:3 NIV)

Pride kills the move of God. It is a most dangerous and sinister invader of relationships on every level, tearing apart families, churches, businesses and close friendships. It opens the door to deception and delusion, leaving destruction and bewilderment in its wake. Think of it as a demonic tornado, changing the landscape from order and peace to disorder and pain.

Why is it so terrible? Why does God hate pride so much? Charles Bridges put it like this: "Pride contends for supremacy with God." In other words, when pride fills the heart it is as if human beings see themselves on a par with God rather than being dependent on Him. The Bible is clear that it is exceedingly offensive to the Lord when we live this way (Proverbs 16:5). It then leads God to resist the proud (James 4:6) and favour the humble.

The opposite of pride is humility. This is our weapon of choice and it will attract the gaze of God towards us. Pride does not simply disappear on its own, because it is part of human nature to be self-centred and look at the world though our own perspective. But humble people learn to look at the world through the eyes of others and are willing to be shaped by trusted friends.

Make your choice

I believe that when we let the fire of God purge our pride, we will know extraordinary power. Jesus loves to inhabit the praises of His people and when we take away the adulation from ourselves and lift it to Him, the Holy Spirit will visit us in a new way. One of the best ways to nail the pride is to spend time worshipping the One who gave you your life. Acknowledge your need of Him, your love for Him and your desire for Him. Kneel at His feet and call Him King of Kings and Lord of Lords. Take time to place Him in the highest place in your life.

You will find that He draws close to you in these moments, filling you with His affection and love. Everything will fall into place. His love will burn in your heart and you will sing with the hymnwriter:

When I survey the wondrous cross
On which the Prince of glory died,
My richest gain I count but loss,
And pour contempt on all my pride.
(Isaac Watts)

Pause for reflection...

• Misplaced pride is at the root of one of the scourges of modern society – a sense of entitlement. Reflect on the example of Jesus who, though He was God in human form, lay aside His own agenda and feelings, and humbled Himself, even to the point of sacrificing His life. Understanding the magnitude of what Christ has done for us puts our pride into perspective.

"It is a great thing when I discover I am no longer my own but His. If the ten shillings in my pocket belong to me, then I have full authority over them. But if they belong to another who has committed them to me in trust, then I cannot buy what I please with them, and I dare not lose them. Real Christian life begins with knowing this."
–Watchman Nee

24

FIRE QUENCHERS: UNFORGIVENESS

—·—

"Yet God, in his grace, freely makes us right in his sight.
He did this through Christ Jesus when he freed us from the
penalty for our sins."
(Romans 3:24 NLT)

—·—

Not one of us deserves the grace of God. It is only because we have been forgiven and set free through the cross of Jesus that we can live as we do. He is our ultimate example and by His Spirit we can also, and should also, forgive others (Ephesians 4:32).

Unforgiveness is like a cancer which grows inside a person and affects not just the individual, but everyone close to them. I have witnessed whole families affected by the bitter root of unforgiveness in just one member. The Bible warns us about exactly that: *"See to it that no one misses the grace of God and that no bitter root grows up to cause trouble and defile many"* (Hebrews 12:15). When pain, disappointment and rejection cause damage to a person, they can either hold onto it, or release it to God and receive healing.

Let me warn you that forgiveness is not easy. We feel justified in repaying the evil done to us with coldness and hardness of heart. Everything in us cries, *why shouldn't I?* We want to keep the other party in bondage to their wrongdoing because it makes us feel as if we have gained some control of the situation. We want to keep the offence before us, vowing never to be hurt like that again.

The harsh reality is that we cannot be truly free this way and all the time, our flame is dying.

Make your choice

I believe that God wants to help you make the choice to forgive. You don't have to do it on your own because He will lead you. Yes, it will be hard, but once you make the initial choice, follow it with a faith confession: I forgive them Father. It may take time for your heart and mind to be healed, but be reassured that the Holy Spirit is doing a deep and hidden work in you. Forgiving someone does not require a fake relationship with them in future; keep it real, but allow the Holy Spirit to change you so that the sting disappears and your heart grows soft again.

Pray with me:

Father, help me to make the right choice to forgive. I am here today because Jesus forgave me. I want to live in freedom and be an example of Your love everywhere I go. Amen.

Pause for reflection...

• If you have been wounded deeply by someone in your life, and you're finding it difficult to forgive, keep going back to God and keep speaking out your forgiveness and asking for further healing. Forgiveness is frequently a process and can take time to work out. But your confession is powerful and you can be sure that God is releasing healing deep within.

25

FIRE QUENCHERS: ISOLATION

———.———

"Let us think of ways to motivate one another to acts of love
and good works. And let us not neglect our meeting together,
as some people do, but encourage one another, especially now
that the day of his return is drawing near."
(Hebrews 10:24-25 NLT)

———.———

God is relational. He is triune which means He is three parts in one and each member, Father, Son and Holy Spirit are in relationship with one another. When Jesus came to earth, He was born into a family, with brothers and sisters, and when He began His ministry He lived in community with His disciples. God has never functioned in isolation and neither must we. Working and living entirely on our own limits our effectiveness and fruitfulness.

Christians need to live in the context of community with other Christians, sharing and doing life together. The Bible is clear that not only must we love the Lord with all our heart and soul and mind, but we must love the person next to us as much as we love ourselves (Matthew 22:37-40).

I don't know everything and neither do you! I need people to help me on my journey and I love to see others exhibit their individual gifts, which are not the same as my own. The Lord has set things up in such a way that we need one another, which the enemy hates because being in community helps us to grow.

Discouragement and doubt kick in when we are isolated and one key strategy of the enemy is to cause division on every possible level of relationship. Be aware of this and order your life in such a way that you live in the context of true community.

Make your choice

It is not always easy to make ourselves accountable to one another. It requires trust, especially when someone speaks words of truth which we may find difficult to receive. True relationships that are built on the Word of God and the grace of the Holy Spirit will keep us healthy (Ephesians 4:15-16). It requires us to be mature and compassionate and we should avoid soulish connections which tend to be built on emotional dysfunction rather than Jesus' example.

Remember that when God created Adam He said, *"It is not good that man should be alone"* (Genesis 2:18) so He gave him Eve for company. Where do you belong? Are your relationships helping you grow in faith and fire? Are you helping others in the same way? If you are isolated, either by choice or design, it is time to pray that God will lead you into community.

Pause for reflection...

• We've learnt that solitude is not the same as isolation. It's beneficial to spend time alone with God regularly. But isolation is counter-productive, because we have been designed to live in community with others. Today, take an inventory of your life and make sure that you are connected with others in various spheres of life. We need to nurture *substantial*, rather than *superficial*, relationships with others that help strengthen our spiritual life.

"Let him who cannot be alone beware of community ... Let him who is not in community beware of being alone ... Each by itself has profound perils and pitfalls. One who wants fellowship without solitude plunges into the void of words and feelings, and the one who seeks solitude without fellowship perishes in the abyss of vanity, self-infatuation and despair."
–Dietrich Bonhoeffer

26
FIRE QUENCHERS: THE SPIRIT OF THE AGE

"Take delight in the Lord,
and he will give you your heart's desires.."
(Psalm 37:4 NLT)

The term, "spirit of the age" refers to the way the world around us thinks, operates, builds friendships, views money and conducts relationships. When we come to Christ, we are called out of the value system of the world and into God's Kingdom values. In the Bible, Paul describes it this way: *"But the fruit of the Spirit is love, joy, peace, forbearance, kindness, goodness, faithfulness, gentleness and self-control. Against such things there is no law"* (Galatians 5:22-23). In other words, being a Christian means we are frequently called to live life the opposite way to that of the world.

Many people work hard to play hard. I am not against all forms of entertainment, but if all we do is earn money to serve our own desires, we become dulled to kindness, goodness and self-control. If we give in to selfishness, we forget how to love others, and if we become immersed in self-gratification of any kind, we can slip away from faithfulness and into infidelity. More than ever before it is vital to make a stand against the evil in our world. As Christians, we need to be very careful not to become so "culturally relevant" that we offend the cross of Christ.

Make your choice

Wherever the values of God's kingdom clash with those of the world, we need to make a strong choice to remain focused. No one ever said that a radical Christian life would be easy, but we must stand firm in the truth that anyone who befriends the world makes an enemy of God (James 4:4-5). It doesn't mean we must live a miserable or segregated life, far from it! God has given us everything to enjoy and His world is full of beauty (1 Timothy 6:17).

But deep down, we know when we are straying from life and into death, because of the unpleasant and miserable effect it has on us. If the fire in your heart is quenched, ask yourself why. If you have lost intimacy with Jesus, is it time to turn off the TV and open your Bible?

Pause for reflection...

• We all need to learn to guard our hearts and protect what enters our soul. Fight for the health of your inner life and ask the Holy Spirit to give you the courage and strength you need to press on towards that prize which is so much more precious than gold.

• We don't need to go around feeling guilty all the time – God has given us life to enjoy. But we are to enjoy life *with Him*, so we need to beware of so-called pleasures that drag us away from Him.

"The greatest enemy of hunger for God is not poison but apple pie. It is not the banquet of the wicked that dulls our appetite for heaven, but endless nibbling at the table of the world."
–John Piper

27
A PSALM OF PROMISE

——•——

"This I declare about the Lord:
He alone is my refuge, my place of safety;
he is my God, and I trust him."
(Psalm 91:2 NLT)

——•——

I believe that God wants to encourage us to hold fast to Him in these days. Many exciting things are ahead for us all.

We have considered those things that seek to quench the fire in our hearts and have learned how to stay strong and not be distracted from the road ahead. Now let's take time to open our hearts to His Word together and allow the truth to set a seal on those things.

Open your Bible at Psalm 91.

Pray that God will draw near to you as you read it, speaking truth and fresh revelation into your heart.

This psalm is full of promise.

It tells us we can shelter next to God and be at rest. It paints a vivid picture of the shadow of God over us as protection and refuge. Not only that, but God will save us from traps left for us by the enemy and keep us healthy by spreading His wings over us. It reminds us how faithful He is, meaning that we can take courage and not be worried or afraid by things that come at us, day or night. We learn that we don't have to fear that what happens to other people will happen to us, because God is with us all the time. When we are intentional about putting God first, the psalm encourages us that we will avoid disaster and harm because we have the added protection of the angels, who He sends to guard us and lift us up. When everything is in the right order, we are able to win battles against demonic forces that would have previously destroyed us. God knows when we love Him first, and He promises to protect us, answer our prayers, comfort us when times are hard, deliver us from oppression. He will even honour us with a long and complete life.

Thank You

We mustn't forget to thank God for His promises to us. Whatever else we do to keep the fire burning, it is all in the context of God's love for us, which came first. His promises have endured from before time began and will continue into eternity. Nothing we do will change the truth contained within these verses.

Pause for reflection...

• Take time now to express your gratitude to your Father who loves you. Thank Him for His protection over your life. Whenever you feel as though you are under attack, make a habit of sheltering under the wing of God's presence and trust Him to be your deliverer and protector.

• Take a few verses of this psalm at a time and commit them to memory. Spend time meditating on the truths the verses contain and allow that truth to embed itself in your heart.

"With time you can learn where to go for nourishment, where to hide for protection, where to turn for guidance. Just as your earthly house is a place of refuge, so God's house is a place of peace." –Max Lucado

28
THE PLACE OF PEACE

"And let the peace that comes from Christ rule in your hearts.
For as members of one body you are called to live in peace.
And always be thankful."

(Colossians 3:15 NLT)

Do you remember the story where Jesus and His disciples boarded a boat to cross the lake and a huge storm whipped up? The Bible describes it as *furious*, with waves so high they were completely overwhelming. The disciples were terrified that they were about to drown, but Jesus took authority over the storm and peace descended (Matthew 8:23-27).

Even though we are living in exciting, hope-filled days, there is also an increase in dark, demonic storms which threaten to steal our peace. Clashes between the kingdoms of heaven and hell are becoming more intense and apparent on every level and it is natural to feel afraid. Let me encourage you that there is an antidote to fear and it is the peace that comes when we stay close to Jesus.

"You will keep in perfect peace all who trust in you, all whose thoughts are fixed on you." (Isaiah 26:3)

The safest place to live and abide when the storms are raging around us is in the secret place of the Most High God. It is a place of protection and peace where the enemy can't draw us out or touch us. On the boat, Jesus challenged His disciples for their lack of faith. It was clear that because they were next to Him, there was no need to fear, even if circumstances looked bleak and logic told them they were about to drown. The peace of God isn't reserved for those times when everything is calm; it is available within and despite the storms we go through.

Imitate Jesus

When Jesus stopped the storm in its tracks, it was not because He wanted to behave like a glitzy magician in a show. Jesus never operated like that. There was no trickery and He had no desire for admiration or applause. It had everything to do with setting an example. In this one moment, Jesus demonstrated clearly how to approach situations which strike fear into our hearts. He didn't leave the storm to rage, but rebuked it. He took authority over it and told it to be quiet. His example is our lifeline when we face situations which steal our peace. Many people struggle with crippling fear about all manner of things and, as followers of Jesus, we need to live in such a way that our lives display the opposite.

Pause for reflection...

• What are the things that regularly steal your peace? Worrying about money, your job, your family, your health? Whatever the issue is, bring it to God today. Place it in His hands and ask Him to fill you with His peace in exchange. God doesn't want us to live hounded by fear. Instead we need to learn to trust Him wholeheartedly. The more we trust, the less we fear.

"If I could hear Christ praying for me in the next room, I would not fear a million enemies. Yet distance makes no difference. He is praying for me."
–Robert Murray McCheyne

29
THE PLACE OF REST

—·—

"Are you tired? Worn out? ... Come to me. Get away with me
and you'll recover your life. I'll show you how to take a real
rest. Walk with me and work with me – watch how I do it.
Learn the unforced rhythms of grace."
(Matthew 11:28 MSG)

—·—

It is possible to be in a place of rest even when you are busy.
Jesus worked extremely hard during His three years of ministry
– travelling many miles healing the sick, delivering people
from oppression and teaching about the Kingdom of God. But
it is clear from the gospel accounts that He didn't minister in a
frantic or stressed way. Rather, He knew how to operate from
a place of rest.

When we encounter a person who rushes around, always
early or always late, breathless with so many jobs on their to-
do list, we tend to back away so as not to absorb their stress.
In contrast, we are drawn to people who are calm and restful,
because despite their busyness they have learned how to
prioritise.

People were drawn to the compassion and love of Jesus.
Frequently surrounded by crowds of people in the heat of
the day, it would have been easy for Jesus to become short-
tempered or dismissive. But He lived in rest. Let me remind
you of the story about the woman who needed healing in Luke
8:43-48. The only way she felt she could receive it in the middle
of a huge crowd was to touch the hem of Jesus' cloak. While

He was being jostled and pushed by people demanding this and that, Jesus stopped and asked, "Who touched me?" The woman came forward and not only was she healed, but Jesus took the time to listen to her story. He restored her dignity as well as her body.

Imitate Jesus

Living in a place of rest is not easy, but the Holy Spirit helps us. Being busy while at rest sounds like a contradiction, but it is exactly how Jesus lived. He showed us how to be active and burn with the love of God without burning out.

The key thing is to stay close to the Father.

I have found this to be a very important discipline in my own life as ministry has required more of my time and energy.

Let me encourage you to not fall into the trap of being busy for the sake of it. Sometimes, frantic activity gives us a sense of worth and importance. We need to remember that our value comes from being a child of God and not what we do. Jesus never forgot who His Father was and, in the same way, we need to rest in Him and let Him lead us through our life and ministry.

Pause for reflection...

• It's been said often that we are valued for who we are, not what we do, but it bears repeating because we regularly slip into the trap of trying to perform to earn God's love and favour. Today, meditate on the fact that you can do nothing to earn God's love – you already have it. This is the starting point for a life that works from a place of rest, rather than resting from work.

30
ONE LIFE

"Give thanks to the Lord, for he is good.
His love endures for ever."
(Psalm 136:1 NLT)

We only get one life! There are no second chances. We may be fortunate to live to 100, or we may not, but more important than the years we are alive is how well we live them. The definition of a highly flammable life is not how many people we preach to, or how many miles we travel, but how devoted to Jesus we are.

Let me tell you the stories of two very different missionaries.

David Brainerd (1718-1747) was a famous American missionary to the Native Indians. He only lived for 29 years. During his life, he only won a few converts, never travelled overseas, never married and was not well known. But he would write journals filled with records of his struggles, passions, victories and weaknesses – and it was these writings that went on to inspire great pioneers of the faith such as Jonathan Edwards and William Carey. These men and others went on to impact countless millions of lives in their lifetime.

John Wesley (1703-1791) on the other hand, lived for 87 years and, with fire in his heart, travelled up and down England preaching to everyone he met and leading thousands to Christ. He was the father of the Methodist movement which spread across the world and is still active today.

God is looking for you

There are things you can do which no one else can. God has made you as you are, in His image (Genesis 1:27) with the potential to be a world-changer. All He is looking for is a heart that says *yes*. He is not restricted by your situation, your health, your finances or your past. There is nothing that can separate you from His love (Romans 8:38-39) and the power that comes to change you and the world around you. He uses men, women and children of every race, intellect, experience and situation to fulfil His purposes. I find this so exciting, because there is no hierarchy in the Kingdom of God.

Often, it is unlikely people who attract God's attention. The Bible tells of Jacob who walked with a limp, Gideon who was scared a lot of the time, Samson who was spoilt and Mary Magdalene who had lived an immoral life. The list goes on. Never think you are redundant or unknown to your Heavenly Father. He sees you and has big dreams to share with you if you will let Him.

Pause for reflection...

• It's tempting to compare ourselves to others and think, "What good can I do?" But the truth is, your life speaks to those in your circle of influence, and you are uniquely made to reach people no one else can. God has also given you unique gifts and abilities that He can use for His purposes. Pray and ask God today to use you for His glory and to take you on an adventure of faith.

"Refuse to be average.
Let your heart soar as
high as it will."
–A.W. Tozer

31
WINDOWS OF OPPORTUNITY

—•—

*"Yet who knows whether you have come to the kingdom for
such a time as this?"*

(Esther 4:14 NLT)

—•—

Just as there are seasons in the natural world, so there are times
and seasons in the Spirit when God urges us to press forward
and not falter. In the New Testament, the Greek word *kairos* is
used to describe a "window of opportunity" in time; a moment
that will not exist forever, and which has the mark of God's
favour upon it. A *kairos* moment requires courage to act. God
wants to achieve great things through us, but if we ignore these
moments to act through laziness, fear or coldness, we may
never get another chance.

As I reflect on my own life, I can identify numbers of missed
opportunities which became "what ifs". Let me encourage you
to align your heart closely to the heartbeat of God, so that you
recognise these unique moments, initiated by Him, weighted
with purpose. Let us not become a people of apathy, but an
army of fire-breathers, passionate in our pursuit of victory for
our Lord Jesus.

David was a simple shepherd boy and the youngest in his
family. His brothers were swarthy soldiers, fighting battles
while he sat high in the hills watching sheep and composing
music. But when he stood before Goliath, the calm certainty
of who he was and what he was called to do filled him with
fiery courage, and he felled the giant with a sling and a

stone (1 Samuel 17:48-49). What a remarkable testimony to the supernatural power of God and the obedience of this teenage boy. A window of opportunity had opened and David embraced it out of his devotion to the Lord.

Listen to the Holy Spirit

God is always looking for people through whom He can demonstrate His power. Our world is full of demonic "giants" that intimidate and harass people of every race, social strata, age and gender. Like David we need to step forward and face the enemy for ourselves and for others. It will mean we must listen to what the Holy Spirit is saying and accept that He may ask us to do out of the ordinary things. David overcame Goliath not with armour and a sword, but with a sling and a stone in the power of the Almighty God. Imagine what would have happened if David had ignored this moment?

Let's be ready to partner with Jesus and step out into new realms of the miraculous.

Pause for reflection...

• I want to encourage you to become bolder in your walk with God. Ask the Holy Spirit to make you alert to those *kairos* moments, and be prepared to step out in faith. It may be something as simple as initiating a conversation or offering to pray for someone who is ill or in distress. Through these simple acts of obedience, God can do amazing things.

32
CREATED FOR PURPOSE

—·—

"Give thanks to the Lord, for he is good.
His love endures for ever."

(Psalm 136:1 NLT)

—·—

There is no greater tragedy than an unfulfilled life and unrealised potential. Jesus provides us with the greatest example of purpose and a destiny fulfilled. He lived His life "on purpose", spending time listening to what God was saying, watching what God was doing and then acting in the power of the Holy Spirit. In the same way, we discover more about our purpose in life through intimacy with God. The closer we walk with Him, the more He will reveal to us about who we are and what we are meant to do.

Every one of us is created for purpose. Life is full of promise and potential and God delights in partnering with us as we discover what it is we are here to do. One of the greatest keys to knowing why we are here on earth is to learn to keep waiting and work faithfully until God is ready to act. Our destiny is not suddenly going to fall out of the sky and drop into our laps regardless of how we live, because God watches how we stay faithful in the small, simple things. The Bible is full of testimonies about men and women who worked hard, stayed open and humble, and made room for change. God promoted people like Joseph who served in a prison (Genesis 40:4) and Moses who looked after sheep in the wilderness (Exodus 3:1). Laziness and arrogance are not character traits that attract the

Holy Spirit, because God needs to trust us to work with Him and walk with Him in humility and obedience.

Stay close

If you want to know what it is that God wants you to do, let me encourage you to work at intimacy with Him. It is when we draw close to Jesus that we discover our destiny and identity. The enemy wants to make us flustered and anxious that we will miss out on God's glory. But the truth is, the closer we become to Him, the more revelation we receive. There may be things in your past that you have always done, that you will no longer need to do. There may be places you will go that you have never been, meeting people you don't yet know. Anything is possible! Just remain faithful and keep close.

"But as for me, it is good to be near God." (Psalm 73:28)

Pause for reflection...

• God created you with a specific purpose in mind and gave you particular gifts and abilities to enhance and support that purpose. If you are unclear about exactly how to pursue your purpose, make time to be alone with God. Spend time in His presence just worshipping Him, and also in silence, listening for His voice. The more time you spend in that secret place, the more revelation you will receive about what God wants you to do. Be obedient and allow the Holy Spirit to lead you, step by step.

"Our greatest fear
should not be of failure,
but of succeeding at
things in life that don't
really matter."
–Francis Chan

33

WHEN GOD FANS THE FLAME

—————•—————

"God's love has been poured out into our hearts through the
Holy Spirit, who has been given to us ... at just the right time,
when we were still powerless, Christ died for the ungodly.
(Romans 5:5-6 NIV)

—————•—————

At times God will accelerate His work in our lives. It may be
that He wants to use us in a particular way, or there may be
situations around us that require an urgent visitation of His
Spirit. After months and years of waiting, we experience a
fresh wave of God's presence. Our vision and passion return
and our tiredness and longing melts away.

The book of Acts tells of the spread of the Gospel following
Jesus' ascent into heaven. At the start of the book, the disciples
and some others were all in one room, wondering what was
going to happen next. They knew about the Holy Spirit and
Jesus had promised them they wouldn't be left alone (John
14:18), but all they could do was pray and wait. When a sudden
violent wind filled the room,

"...they saw what seemed to be tongues of fire that separated
and came to rest on each of them. All of them were filled with
the Holy Spirit and began to speak in other tongues as the Spirit
enabled them." (Acts 2:3-4)

Following this dramatic encounter, the Gospel exploded
and the disciples experienced a whole new level of miraculous
power.

Heaven's bellows

When air is squeezed into a small fire, the oxygen causes the fire to burn hotter and faster. The flames grow and catch more and more of the combustible materials around it. It is the same with us. When God fans the flame in our hearts, we change and the impact we have on our surroundings is redefined. We begin to expect the miraculous and our faith rises. We have a clearer understanding of our purpose and destiny and, all at once, everything makes sense. People, too, begin noticing the changes and are drawn to the presence of God within us.

God has a unique purpose for every believer and our lives are transformed when we connect with that purpose. I believe we must give God permission to stoke our fire and make us ready. We are in desperate times and the world is crying out for God to come and heal it. When the disciples received the fire of God, they were unstoppable, and the Kingdom of God advanced as never before.

C.T. Studd said, "Oh let my love with fervour burn!"

May the same be true for us today.

Pause for reflection...

• A.W. Tozer wrote that, "The Spirit-filled life is not a special, deluxe edition of Christianity. It is part and parcel of the total plan of God for His people." Today, pray and ask God to fill you afresh with His Spirit, and ask Him to fan the flame of faith in your heart and to re-ignite your passion for Jesus.

34
BECOMING MORE LIKE JESUS

———·———

*"In that day you will know that I am in My Father, and you
in Me, and I in you."*
(John 14:20 NKJV)

———·———

As we walk with Jesus, we should become more and more like
Him as time goes on. God's plan for us is that we grow and
mature continually, being shaped into His Son's likeness. It is
less about what we do and more about who we are. Francis
Frangipane describes how God feels about this:

"What pleases the Father most is not what proceeds from
our hands but what rises from our hearts."

Living a highly flammable life requires our commitment
to *transformation* before *function*. In other words, we should
put Jesus before all other activity, process, programmes or
enterprise, however worthy or noble they are.

When Paul wrote to the Christians in Galatia he said,

*"My dear children, for whom I am again in the pains of
childbirth until Christ is formed in you."* (Galatians 4:19)

Paul had a deep longing for these believers to look, talk and
act like Jesus, manifesting the nature and character of God to
everyone around them.

Authentic faith

If we are to expect change in others, we need to have
experienced change for ourselves. The way of Jesus is one of
example. In other words, it was from His relationship with

God that all things flowed and He remained committed to His Father to the cross and beyond. There is no room for duality in the life of a burning one. We must allow Christ to be fully formed in us and stay close to the ways of Jesus by studying and imitating Him. We need to recognise that this will result in the reshaping of our character, which can be painful at times, but we can trust God to lead the process with love and care.

The process of becoming more like Jesus is sometimes simple, sometimes complex. We would not expect to go to the gym and be super-fit in a day, as it takes time to build up muscle and stamina. There will be some aspects of the workout that are more difficult than others, but the end goal will be achieved in time. The pursuit of an authentic faith requires the same discipline. Prayer, Bible study, worship and time with other Christians are foundational to a transformed life as we allow the Holy Spirit to breathe into our lives and change us for good.

Let's be intentional in our pursuit of an authentic, Jesus-centred life which glorifies God.

Pause for reflection...

• We tend to resist any kind of change which might disrupt our comfort zones, but change is inevitable and especially so in the Christian life. In a year's time, we shouldn't be the same people we are today, because God will have transformed our hearts a bit more and moved us on in our journey. Reflect on this today and aim to cooperate with God's work in your life, embracing rather than resisting the changes He wants to bring for your benefit.

When it is a question of
God's almighty Spirit.
Never say, I can't."
–Oswald Chambers

35
SPREADING THE FIRE

"Looking at them, Jesus said, 'With people it is impossible, but not with God; for all things are possible with God.'"
(Mark 10:27 NASB)

We are called to make disciples for Jesus in every nation on earth (Matthew 28:18-20). There is no opt-out clause to Jesus' command, so we must consider what we are doing to fulfil it. Is it something we are passionate about or does the very thought of it make us anxious? Perhaps life is so busy there is no spare time to tell people about Jesus?

Remember that we are being transformed daily to become more like our Lord. Evangelism will therefore be less about a dry or awkward presentation of the Gospel and much more about the contagious and wonderful presence of Jesus who dwells in our hearts. When people encounter us, they will come face to face with the Holy Spirit within and the fire will spread. The Bible tells us that signs and wonders will accompany those who believe (Mark 16:17) and people will be healed, set free and cleansed, pointing to the truth of God's love and the promise of salvation for all who receive Him. Expect God to use you this way!

Smith Wigglesworth was once travelling by train and had sat quietly for some time. Suddenly, the man sitting behind him jumped up and shouted at him, "You're convicting me of my sin!" How could this happen? It was simply that Wigglesworth carried so much of the presence of God that it affected those who encountered him.

No more niceties

Being overly nice is the curse of our time. It is a form of political correctness born from a fear of being offensive or rude. We think that if we make everything bland, we will be accepted and avoid conflict. Let me remind you that being a Christian was never supposed to be an easy ride. Jesus said plainly that people would openly hate us and persecute us for His sake (Matthew 10:22), so we are challenged to rise up and be different. Jesus was never nice! It is impossible to burn with the fire of God and settle for anything other than boldness and courage as we let the flames burn brightly through our lives. The time for being a nice church is over. It is time for God's people to move forward and make a difference.

Let's mobilise ourselves and win the lost for the One who paid the price for the world He loves.

Pause for reflection...

• I don't know about you, but I long to be so full of God's presence that people notice and it affects them, even before I've opened my mouth. I pray that you would be filled with more of God's presence today, and that it would result in a divine boldness and courage to reach out to others with His love and compassion.

36
WHAT'S PAST HAS PASSED

"But to all who believed him and accepted him, he gave the
right to become children of God."
(John 1:12 NLT)

We all have different backgrounds and our childhoods are unique. You may have grown up in a safe, loving family and be very secure in your identity. Or perhaps you have experienced a dysfunctional or abusive upbringing where you received little or no affirmation? Whichever is true for you, let me encourage you that God has chosen you and you were not born by mistake. So many people struggle to shake off the legacy of their childhood and stay bound to the lies the enemy tells them that they will never make a difference in the world because of what happened to them.

In the Bible, God speaks through the prophet Jeremiah, saying,

"Before I shaped you in the womb, I knew all about you. Before you saw the light of day, I had holy plans for you." (Jeremiah 1:5)

This means He was there from the beginning, creating you, watching over you, nurturing you and dreaming about all the great things you would do with Him in the future. At no point is there any talk of disqualification from your purpose because of your past. Nothing that has been done or not done can keep Jesus away, so it is time to embrace the truth and cut any ties from the past that are stopping the pursuit into your destiny.

The Good News

The most compassionate people often turn out to be the ones who have gone through difficult circumstances. The good news is that not only does God heal us of our past, He also uses us to soothe and comfort those who have known the same pains who haven't yet met Jesus. So, while we must leave the sting of our own past at the cross, we can, in the power of the Holy Spirit, use what we have gone through to bless and lead others into healing. Miracles happen in those quiet moments when a person in pain can trust us to listen and lead them into an encounter with the Lord.

Let's take these verses to heart today:

"Praise be to the God and Father of our Lord Jesus Christ, the Father of compassion and the God of all comfort, who comforts us in all our troubles, so that we can comfort those in any trouble with the comfort we ourselves receive from God." (2 Corinthians 1:3-4)

Pause for reflection...

• We all have a history, some of it good, some of it bad. But here is the truth: nothing you've done in your past has disqualified you from the grace of God in this present moment and in the future. Our Father is the great redeemer, the One who is constantly taking broken vessels, filling them with His love and power, and using them to accomplish His purposes. All you have to do is cooperate.

"When we stray from His presence, He longs for you to come back. He weeps that you are missing out on His love, protection and provision. He throws His arms open, runs toward you, gathers you up, and welcomes you home."
–Charles Stanley

37
INSPIRATIONAL LIVES

"Whatever you do, do it all for the glory of God."
(1 Corinthians 10:31 NLT)

When people burn with passion for something, they are usually compelled to take action and make a difference. Some people I know are passionate about justice and so become lawyers. Others are committed to rescuing children and teenagers from slavery, while others have a vision to become teachers, nurses or doctors. Inside us all is the potential to set the world on fire. When we see things happening in our world and feel strongly that someone should do something about it, that person is likely to be us! God will plant varied seeds of desire in all of us to prompt us to make a difference in our surrounding environment and beyond. The Holy Spirit will then lead us to act by opening doors.

Imagine what Calcutta would be like had Mother Teresa not responded to the ache in her heart on seeing the millions of sick and dying in India. Turned down three times by the authorities when she put in a request to be a missionary, she persisted in prayer and fasting and writing to the authorities until she was granted permission. She went on to found the "Missionaries of Charity" changing the lives of millions for the better.

Think of William Wilberforce who, three hundred years ago, with fire in his soul, led a quest to see slavery abolished forever. He fought for it his entire life and a few days before his death, learned that the Bill for the Abolition of Slavery would be passed in the House of Lords.

What is your fire?

We are created to love and be loved. We are not robots, devoid of feeling or empathy, destined to sit around to live functional and utilitarian lives. God has made us in His image and we are to burn with the same things He cares about.

So, what is it that catches fire within you? What moves you to tears or righteous anger? Do you have an inkling that God is calling you into something radical for Him?

To be inspired by the lives of those who have made a difference in the world is vital, as it builds faith and hope for our own future with Jesus. Anything is possible with God (Matthew 19:26), so let me encourage you to take time to consider what the world would look like if you and Jesus partnered together in something extraordinary.

Pause for reflection...

• What is your passion? What is it that causes you to want to take action? What really motivates you? Think about how God might use the things you're passionate about, surrendered to Him, to make a difference in your world.

38
LEARNING TO SERVE

—•—

"It is absolutely clear that God has called you to a free life. Just make sure that you don't use this freedom as an excuse to do whatever you want to do and destroy your freedom. Rather, use your freedom to serve one another in love; that's how freedom grows."
(Galatians 5:13 MSG)

—•—

In the New Testament, the same word is used in the Greek for both "ministry" and "serving". Therefore, whatever it is we do in life will be less about platforms or being well known and much more about understanding sacrifice. This means we need to learn to become *hidden* and wait for God to promote us in His time and His way.

The life of Jesus is a wonderful example of a life lived to serve others. In Him there was no arrogance, no jostling for position or recognition. In fact, it was often the opposite. He would instruct people to say nothing about their healing to anyone in order to deflect attention away from Himself (Mark 1:43-44). Jesus was clear about the fact that He was on earth to serve His Father's purposes (John 12:27) and do what His Father was doing (John 5:19-20).

These days, we see so many teaching materials dedicated to self-development and how to climb up the career ladder. Whilst there is nothing inherently wrong with living a full and active life, we are not called to put ourselves at the centre of it. It is Jesus who should be at the centre.

Test yourself

The best way to know what we really think about a life of service and sacrifice is to see how we deal with mundane and thankless tasks. It is easy to be resentful if we are asked to put out the chairs instead of leading a meeting, because we are waiting for that moment when the world will finally see how amazing we are on a platform! The truth is that we are called by God to get on with the "here and now" until such time that He directs us more specifically into something else. Living a highly flammable life will always have a dimension of service to it because we are God's workmanship, created in Christ to do good works (Ephesians 2:10). If our pride stands in the way of accepting menial tasks, we are not ready to be trusted with more.

So, the next time you are asked to do something you feel is beneath you, examine your heart. Look beyond any pride or resistance, and instead echo the words of Jesus who said:

"I have brought You glory on earth by completing the work You gave me to do." (John 17:4)

Pause for reflection...

• Jesus never strived to be seen or heard, He just did whatever He saw God the Father doing. He wasn't concerned about position or affirmation, but rested secure in the affirmation of His Father. In the same way, let's seek to serve God and others with humility, seeking to bring glory to Him.

• If you feel called to do something for God, but it doesn't seem to be happening yet, keep serving patiently, don't lose heart, and keep trusting God to bring your dreams to fruition.

My trust in God flows out of the experience of his loving me, day in and day out, whether the day is stormy or fair, whether I'm sick or in good health, whether I'm in a state of grace or disgrace. He comes to me where I live and loves me as I am.
–Brennan Manning

39
SURPRISES IN STORE

———•———

"But you, O Lord, are a shield around me;
you are my glory, the one who holds my head high."
(Psalm 3:3 NLT)

———•———

Walking with God is an adventure. Jesus came to show us how to live a life rooted in intimacy with the Father and burning with the fire of His presence. The miracles, signs and wonders flowed from that place of devotion and love to show us how much God loves His world. As we walk the journey into discovering our destiny, we need to devote our lives to His ways.

There will be times when God decides to surprise us, taking us out of our comfort zone and changing our perspective. It shakes us and reminds us that all we see in the physical world is not all there is. It is therefore important that we trust God completely and learn to lean not on our own understanding but on His leading.

Luke 24 tells us the story of two disciples whose hearts were heavy and broken because they had seen Jesus die on the cross. All their hopes and dreams had been placed on Him, so His death was a catastrophic blow to their faith. But when a stranger joined them on a walk to Emmaus from Jerusalem and spoke to them from the Scriptures, it was only afterwards they realised they had been walking with the risen Jesus! Amazed and surprised, they said, *"Did not our hearts burn within us when He talked to us?"* (Luke 24:32)

Hearts on fire

Your heart was created to burn; to overflow with the radiating glory of His presence. It is impossible to walk and talk with God and remain unchanged. He is ready to surprise you with encounters you have never had up to this point; to show you He is with you and has exciting plans for your future together. Meeting Him will make you burn with passion and fire that will change you forever. He restores hope, gives strength to the weary and fills us with love and compassion. Miracles will follow and His kingdom will be established. Let's not allow our limited understanding to quench His presence. Make room for supernatural activity in your life and get ready to be surprised by extraordinary happenings.

"Delight yourself in the Lord and He will give you the desires of your heart. Commit your way to the Lord; trust in Him and He will do this." (Psalm 37:4-5)

Amen! Come, Lord Jesus.

Pause for reflection...

• God never planned for your life to be routine and mundane. Rather, He wants you to learn that by walking with Him, tuned into His voice, your life can be an adventure of ever-deepening trust, filled with supernatural occurrences.

• If you feel that you have lost the passion you once felt, ask Jesus to rekindle that flame and renew your hope.

40
ONE SMALL FLAME

—·—

"Give thanks to the Lord, for he is good.
His faithful love endures for ever."
(Psalm 136:1 NLT)

—·—

At the start of our devotional journey together we learned how Elijah prepared an altar to God which blazed with the fire of heaven, despite being drenched with water. The sign was clear: God can and will do the impossible, even when conditions and circumstances say otherwise.

We know that it takes only one small flame to start a fire. A flickering match has the potential to ignite everything around it and, in the same way, God wants you to be a burning one, igniting the world around you with His presence. You were born for this purpose and it is time to arise and claim your destiny. God knows your heart and has heard your cries for more of Him. He knows you are hungry and thirsty and has promised to transform you from glory to glory (2 Corinthians 3:18). You don't have to be especially qualified to belong to the company of burning hearts that God is raising up. All you need to do is make time each day to pray that He will help your desires align with His and be prepared for encounters with His Spirit that will change and empower you from the inside out.

My prayer is that your heart will be set aflame and it will keep burning for the rest of your life. Get ready for the impossible to become possible. No one is promising that a radical Christian life is easy, but it will never be boring as His Kingdom comes and His will is done on earth as it is in heaven. Then we will see the same as the prophet Isaiah:

"Arise, shine, for your light has come, and the glory of the Lord rises upon you. See, darkness covers the earth and thick darkness is over the peoples, but the Lord rises upon you and His glory appears over you." (Isaiah 6:1-2)

A prayer

Lord God, You are the Lover of my soul and the King of my heart. I want to love as you love, pray as you pray, and Jesus, live as you lived. Burn away those things in my life that are keeping me in the dark. Ignite me with passion and set me on fire so that all those around me will be drawn to the light and warmth of Your presence. For Your glory and fame, Amen.

Pause for reflection...

• As you reflect on the things we've discussed in this book, make plans to change your lifestyle so that you are able to spend more time in God's presence, with time for dialoguing with Him and listening to all He has to say. It is in this secret place with the Father that our destinies are forged and we find the fulfilment we all seek.

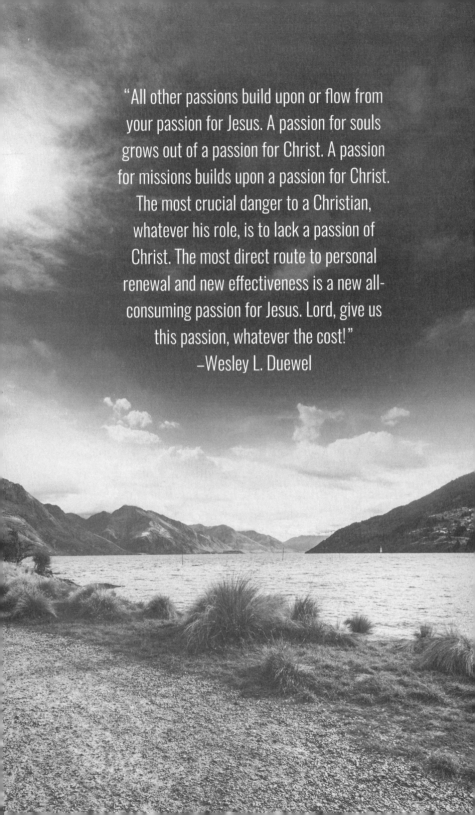

"All other passions build upon or flow from your passion for Jesus. A passion for souls grows out of a passion for Christ. A passion for missions builds upon a passion for Christ. The most crucial danger to a Christian, whatever his role, is to lack a passion of Christ. The most direct route to personal renewal and new effectiveness is a new all-consuming passion for Jesus. Lord, give us this passion, whatever the cost!"

–Wesley L. Duewel